Exeter
in old picture postcards

by Peter Thomas

European Library   ZALTBOMMEL/THE NETHERLANDS

Acknowledgements
I am greatly indebted to Mr. J.R. Cartwright of Exeter for his kindness and assistance with this project.
The West Country Studies Library.
The Department of the Environment.
The Devon and Cornwall Constabulary.
The Exeter Maritime Museum.
The Royal School for the Deaf.

GB ISBN 90 288 2406 5

© 1983 European Library – Zaltbommel/The Netherlands
Second edition, 1997: reprint of the original edition 1983.

No part of this book may be reproduced in any form, by print, photoprint, microfilm or any other means, without written permission from the publisher.

INTRODUCTION

Few people who visit Exeter today can leave without commenting on what an attractive and charming City it is. Certainly it has the reputation of being one of the finest City's in England. Because of its situation on a hill above the river Exe, at the most suitable crossing place for traffic, it has a constant influx of visitors. It is the river to which Exeter owes its existence and it has been a major factor relating to the growth of the City. In times gone by crossing the river was a dangerous business, and long before any bridges were constructed, many lost their lives trying to do so. The site at Exeter gave the securest crossing point. The cliffs at the river's edge had the advantage of providing a natural defence by giving clear views of the surrounding countryside. These basic points for survival came into being many centuries ago and although responsible for shaping the City bears little importance today.

Visitors standing in the centre of Exeter are often surprised to see green fields surrounding the City. This rural aspect is perhaps one of the most charming that Exeter has to offer. Sadly much of that 'untouched' countryside is disappearing as the population increases. The climate of the City is most pleasing being mild for much of the year and this produces a wealth of botanical growth. This has been capitalised upon and today Exeter is recognised as 'The Floral Capital Of Europe'. It boasts some of the oldest public gardens in the country. Centrally situated in one of Englands most beautiful counties, Exeter is an ideal base for travelling around Devon, Cornwall and Dorset. The attractions of Devon are many and thousands of visitors come to absorb its natural beauty. The lure of Dartmoor and Exmoor are strong, being areas of outstanding natural landscape. The ruggedness and wild country of North Devon, the rolling hills and beautiful beaches of South Devon, all add to the passion for exploring the county.

One of the greatest attractions, which dominates the centre of Exeter, is the great Cathedral of St. Peter. Nobody can fail to be impressed by its magnificent structure, which spans a thousand years of the City's history. One of the finest Cathedrals in England, it has the longest Gothic vaulted roof in Europe. This architectural gem has been aptly named 'The Jewel Of The West'. The 'Close' surrounding the Cathedral also contains buildings of historical merit. Mol's Coffee House, St. Martin's Church, The Quadrangle, The Devon and Exeter Institution, The Well House, Tinley's Café and the delightful group of gabled buildings, once used by Cathedral Masons, all add to the character of Exeter. In the High Street stands another priceless treasure, The Guildhall. Its Elizabethan portico straddles the pavement. As the oldest municipal building in the kingdom its history can be traced back to 1154. Its colourful interior reflects the history of the City.

One area which still retains a great deal of interest is 'The West Quarter'. Found here is the famous 'Stepcote Hill', once a main thoroughfare into the City from the river. A steep hill with a multitude of steps, which are cobbled, it is best viewed looking up. It provides a charming vista. At its base stand two restored sixteenth century houses and the ancient church of St. Mary Steps complete with its famous clock 'Matthew the Miller'. Opposite the church is the remains of the old 'West Gate', once part of the City wall. This historic area boasts another unique but introduced piece of history. Situated next to the West Gate stands 'The House That Moved', an early fifteenth century dwelling that was moved in 1961 to save it from demolition. Moved on wheels, it is claimed to be one of the oldest dwelling houses in Europe. Some hundred yards away from the house can be found the remains of the mediaeval Exe Bridge, now part of a landscaped area. The ruin of St. Edmund's Church stands beside the bridge. Within a short distance one can reach the river and the Quay. The leats which operated mills can still be seen. Recently used by BBC television for the series 'The Onedin Line', the Quay provided an authentic backdrop of the period. It was here that much of the trade took place three hundred years ago that led to Exeter's wealth. The main product which was carried from the port was wool, but timber, coffee, tea, wines, spirits, spices, etc. came into the county via the Quay. Trading has long since ceased, but the atmosphere of a maritime port still lingers. At present the Quay area is under analysis for a restoration programme linked with recreation. Over the last decade a different view seems to have been taken by Exeter with regard to retaining more of its past character. As with many City's throughout the country, a great many buildings and areas of historical interest have been lost, but luckily attitudes have changed in Exeter.

This book is based around an often overlooked social document 'The Postcard'. Originating at the turn of the century, postcards were produced on inumerable subjects and by hundreds of photographers throughout the country. Today postcards are mainly produced by large companies and the variety of local cards is generally limited. In the past each town usually had a local photographer who took an interest in local events and would always be available for civic occasions. Local commissions were sometimes granted to record street scenes and the life of the community. The work of a photographer could over a period of years develop into a local archive and contain many irreplaceable records. Postcards being popular were often produced from local records and were a good source of revenue. It is often the more unusual of these records which can be of significant interest to us today. Exeter, not without its share of photographers over the years, has been quite well recorded through the postcard.

For the first time a large number of these cards has been assembled to reflect upon the City between 1880 and 1930. I am sure the residents of Exeter will be intrigued by some of the 'lost views' and in so doing appreciate even more the beauty and historical significance of our 'Ever Faithful City'.

Authors Biography
Mr. Peter Thomas, photographer, writer, lecturer and conservationist, is an Exonian and the owner of the largest private collection of historical photographs relating to Exeter. He is the author of the book 'Old Exeter', the first published photographic study of the pre-war City. The book 'Aspects of Exeter' was also conceived and designed by him and is today classified as a foremost study on Exeter. It was produced in collaboration with Mrs. Jacqueline Warren, a local historian and freelance writer. This publication was presented to His Royal Highness The Prince of Wales in July 1981 and was later displayed at St. James Palace, London. In the same year Mr. Thomas produced and published a booklet on 'The House That Moved'. It was designed to celebrate the twentieth year of its moving. Exhibitions have frequently been arranged on 'Old Exeter', The History of Photography, Natural History, etc. Mr. Thomas has appeared on television and radio and has been interviewed with regard to his publications and his general views on the City and its development.

As a photographer he has always had a strong interest in the 'Natural World' and holds strong views about conservation of the environment. He worked for 'The World Wildlife Fund' on a voluntary basis for number of years as chairman of a regional group in Exeter. He has supplied the Fund with material for educational audio visual projects. His passion for photography is a life time one and very varied. He is the owner of an extensive collection of historical photographic apparatus which relates to the history of photography. He has worked extensively within the retail photographic trade and has a wide knowledge on all its aspects.

As a lecturer he has given talks to universities, colleges, schools, camera clubs, institutes and others. He has travelled extensively and frequently lectures on his experiences abroad.

DOUBLE LOCKS, EXETER

1. In olden days it was possible to navigate the River Exe right up to the City walls and beyond. Because of rivalry with the City, the Earls of Devon blocked the river by constructing a weir which cut the City off from the sea. This led to a substantial loss of revenue for the City. It was therefore decided, in Elizabethan times, to construct a canal to by-pass the River. Initially it went from the Quay at Exeter to Countess wear village. It was however enlarged twice and eventually finished at Turf. Today it is five miles long and fifteen feet deep. It was the first 'Pound Lock' canal in England. The Double Locks Hotel was opened in 1904 and was a favourite meeting place for the Exeter Rowing Club.

2. Residents enjoy the pleasures of the canal. Boats could be hired from Exe Bridge and a pleasant afternoons rowing had for a small fee. The Double Locks Hotel dates from the early eighteenth century and could be the oldest public house built in conjunction with a canal. It is said that the Hotels architecture reflects some Dutch influence.

3. Exeter Canal has always been used for pleasure purposes as well as the more serious trading aspects. The view shown is taken from beside the entrance to Clapperbrook Lane, a charming thoroughfare which led to Alphington Village. The boats would probably have been hired from the Severn Stars Hotel adjacent to Exe Bridge. The owner, Mr. Howard, was an enthusiast and promotor of the Exeter Rowing Club. (Circa 1910.)

4. This scene of Exeter on its hill top overlooking the River Exe has remained almost unchanged for several hundred years. To the right can be seen the spire of St. Leonard's Church, built in 1876. The wooded area and large grey building is the grounds and house known as 'Larkbeare'. The Cathedral of St. Peter, built over a period of a thousand years, dominates the skyline and below it, above the river, is Colleton Crescent. These beautiful Georgian houses stand on the edge of the sandstone cliffs which overlook the river. The spire of St. Mary Majors Church is seen to the left of the Cathedral.

5. The 'Wet Dock' or 'Basin' was constructed to take vessels of a large capacity. The entrance is seen on the left at the top of the Canal while the right is the outlet to the river. Opened on the 29th September 1830, great festivities took place at the Basin to celebrate the occasion. Decorated barges festooned with streamers took quantities of sight seers to the Double Locks and back. Today the 'Basin' is the home of 'The Maritime Museum', one of the world's most comprehensive collections of boats. It is a major tourist attraction. (1907.)

6. 'Moonlight on the Canal' was produced by Raphael Tuck. Taken in daylight it was printed with an overall blue cast rendering a moonlight effect. Horses were utilised on the canal for towing purposes and pulled ships and barges up and down its length. A hard working life for a horse it also had its dangers. On 12th May 1934 a black gelding six years old, which had been purchased by the council in 1928 for £84, was drowned while towing on the canal. The use of horses was abandoned around 1938. (Circa 1903.)

7. This view was recorded from the cliffs of Mount Dinham looking up the River Exe towards St. David's Station. The main road, shown right, is Bonhay Road and leads to the station. The railway bridge ends at a tunnel which brings trains in to Central Station, the nearest station to the City Centre. The bridge over the river was constructed to give a line on the western bank of the river to Newton Abbott, the most popular resort being visited was Dawlish. The line was completed in 1846. The untouched rural hills of Exwick, seen beyond, now carries a substantial housing estate. (Circa 1905.)

8. Cowley Bridge can be found on the Northward road from the City which takes the visitor to Crediton and North Devon. This crossing over the River Exe has probable connections as a Roman crossing place and it was first recorded in 1286. The origin of the name 'Cowley' dates back to Saxon times and means a 'clearing in the woods'.

COUNTESS WEIR, EXETER

9. The delightful village of Countess Wear takes its name from Isabella, Countess of Devon. It was in the year 1284 that the Countess constructed two weirs designed to drive a new mill near Topsham. A gap was left for shipping to pass up to Exeter. However, her successor Hugh De Courtenay blocked the passageway forcing ships to offload at Topsham. The action was to greatly increase the wealth of the Courtenay family and started a battle between the City and the family. The end result was the construction of the Canal to by-pass the river.

COUNTESS WEIR, EXETER

10. Today much of the atmosphere of a rural riverside village has been lost, owing the growth of the Countess Wear. This picturesque view shows the centre of the village around 1920 and was used by local guide books to show a typical village scene that could be found on the outside of the City.

11. Exeter Quay, as we know it today, was mainly constructed in the seventeenth century. Great improvements took place during this time to make Exeter a viable sea port. The warehouses which dominate the Quay were built in 1835. Previously to the railways, being opened in 1844, the port was of vital importance. It was a common sight to see twenty or thirty vessels tied up at the Quay. The most important product handled was coal. Two companies catered for merchandise both having six vessels each which sailed continuously to and fro to London on a weekly basis.

12. On the riverside, Shillhay, seen bottom left, contained much of Exeter's industry prior to the 1960's. The Shillhay is situated between the Higher Leat which runs beside the City Wall and the rivers edge. Within its area could have been found iron foundries, coal merchants, timber yards, tanneries, wine and spirit merchants, garages, millers and others. Today much of the site has been used for dwellings. Many of the buildings shown no longer exist. Behind the Customs House, bottom right, rises Quay Hill which joins West Street. Along its edge can be seen the City Wall. (1925.)

13. The three arched stone bridge was constructed in 1778 and crossed the river from New Bridge Street to St. Thomas. The new bridge collapsed into the river, before completion during a flood. The problem was resolved by relocating the foundations onto solid rock. The cost of construction was £30,000. The bridge was to be demolished in 1904 to make way for a new structure which would allow for a greater flow of traffic, in particular trams. Perhaps the fate of the stone bridge had been sealed when the first vehicle passed over it. It was a hearse!

14. This view of the 1778 bridge is probably the most well known. It has been said that upon its demolition the stone balustrades were removed and placed around the entrance to a large house in Exwick. Shown to the right is a wreck which was a feature of the area for some years. It was probably one of the wooden barges which carried coal and other products up and down the river. (1903.)

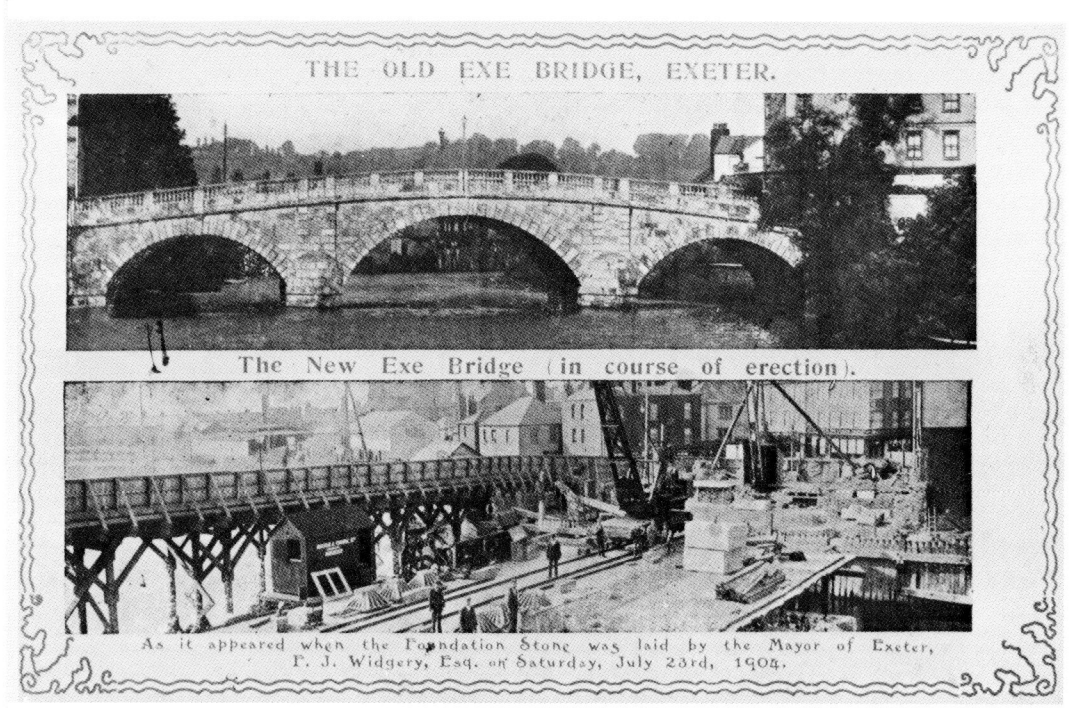

15. A unique souvenir postcard which commemorates the demolition of the stone bridge built 1778 and the laying of the foundation stone for the new iron bridge on Saturday, July 23rd, 1904.

16. The new iron Exe Bridge was opened by Mayor E.C. Perry on 29th March 1905. This grand occasion brought people from all over the City flocking to the new structure. Patriotic flags were hung between its lampposts and a military escort kept thousands of people at bay while the Mayor and Corporation delivered speeches. The opening of the bridge marked the beginning of a new era for Exeter. So enthusiastic was the crowds that Fore Street, Alphington Street, Cowick Street and Okehampton Road were completely blocked. All were waiting to cross the bridge. Onlookers also took up positions on roof tops nearby (see top right).

17. The introduction of the tram into Exeter dates back to around 1880. For twenty years the trams were horse drawn which caused many problems. The advent of the electric tram removed many of these troubles when they were introduced in 1905. The iron bridge was built with trams in mind, being eleven feet wider than its predecessor. The pavements over the bridge were made three feet wider than the previous, which greatly assisted pedestrian traffic. Being a horizontal bridge, not arched, no difficulty was experienced by trams which passed over. The first electric trams were decorated with flags and garlands and came down through the City to the new bridge.

18. Taken from a balcony overlooking the river, next to the Severn Stars Hotel, this postcard shows the wooden pontoon bridge still in position on the other side of the new structure. The pontoon bridge was a temporary measure to assist with building work and to allow passage over the river. It was later removed. Finishing work combining the bridge with New Bridge Street has yet to be completed. (1905.)

19. With access to the City greatly improved the new bridge proved to be a great success. The structure made in cast iron weighed 430 tons. The parapet and ornamental work, a feature of this bridge, added a further 110 tons. To the left overlooking the river is the well known 'Exe Bridge Studio' at this time occupied by the 'Crown Art Company'.

20. One of the most famous accidents that has ever occurred in Exeter was that of the tram crash that ended at Exe Bridge. The tram lost control when coming down over Fore Street and hurtled down the hill. It failed to stop until it was exactly on the bridge itself where it turned over. The accident happened on 7th March 1917. At this time the 'Exe Bridge Studio' was occupied by Mr. Henry Wykes, a well known photographer who started business there in 1912. He recorded the scene from his studio window which overlooked the bridge. Wykes was later to move to Bedford Circus and finally to Northernhay Street.

21. Demolition of some riverside buildings adjacent to the stone bridge allowed new features to appear beside the river. The removal of the Brush factory and other premises made way for a riverside walk. It was to be paved and had ornamental railings along its length. Trees were planted to shade the walker during the warmer summer months. From this vantage point a fine view was to be had of the new bridge. (1910.)

22. From the turn of the century this view remained almost unchanged for a period of sixty years. On the left and adjacent to the bridge was the premises of 'Randall' the seedsman. Amongst his prominent adverts displayed on the shop front was that of the 'British Lion Pea'! It was said that it would outgrow any other that was available and could not be surpassed! Randall's property backed on to the 'Severn Stars Hotel', a resting place for weary travellers, and the site from where theatre originated in the City. The photo is taken from the junction of Cowick Street with Okehampton Street (left). Shown right is the entrance to Gervase Avenue with a horse and cart turning into it. Lower right is Alphington Street.

23. The most prominent feature which has always greeted visitors as they entered the City from St. Thomas is that of the Cathedral which towers above all other buildings. Most of the properties shown in this photograph have been demolished, including the bridge, and the area today bears little resemblence to its former self. The large wall running beside the river shows the edge of Commercial Road with the City Brewery behind. At the junction of Commercial Road and Edmund Street lay the remains of the original mediaeval bridge. The road passed over the top of it. Its position is marked almost exactly by the tree which grows on the rivers edge. The bridge was uncovered in the 1970's and restored, although not all the arches had survived, and today is a tourist attraction.

24. The single span iron bridge stood for seventy years before it was demolished as part of a road improvement plan. Its successors, two precast concrete bridges, unfortunately lack the decor of the former £15,000 iron structure. The construction of an inner by-pass, which carved its way through many of Exeter's historic properties around the West Quarter, was a sad event. Although assisting with increasing the flow of traffic, the City lost some of its most interesting areas. The bridge was part of this loss.

25. Crossing the bridge the visitor found himself in New Bridge Street. This extension to Fore Street was built in 1778 when the City Wall was breached and the road built up to join Exe Bridge. Originally the route into the City was through the West Quarter, but the new street gave direct access to the centre of the City. However one problem was the steepness of Fore Street. Difficulty was often experienced by horses in mounting this last part of the journey. (1907.)

26. 'Backs Hotel', seen left, stood at edge of Exe Bridge and contained within a restaurant. The Hotel was established in 1886 and very often advertised and appeared in City Guides. Adverts read as follows: *Commercial Gentleman and visitors will find this Hotel comfortable and at moderate charges, Trams from all stations, Electric Light, Hot and Cold, Bath.* Behind the Hotel, in Bonhay Road, was the Cattle Market and farmers often frequented the 'Star and Garter' public house which was next door to 'Backs'. A fine lamp hangs outside and underneath the sign reads 'Cranbers Star and Garter'. The Bonhay Road street sign can be seen on the building opposite. (1910.)

27. The joining of New Bridge Street with Fore Street cannot be clearly seen in this record. A tall building halfway up on the left marks the boundary where the two streets meet, and is the corner of Bartholomew Street. This premise was at one time owned by the 'Westlake Brothers', who were grocers. A guide of 1890 highly praises the establishment which began in 1821. Reknowned for their personal service 'Westlake's' ground their own coffee and sold high quality teas. All general provisions were stocked, including quantities of spices, pickles, hams, tinned meats, bacon, cheese, etc. A famous product was 'Westlake's Baking Powder', an original recipe from the proprietor which was highly successful. It was said that it had 'no equals and certainly no superiors'! On the right hand side of New Bridge Street can be seen the balustrades under which flows the Higher Leat. (1906.)

28. West Street branching from Fore Street leads into what is known as 'The West Quarter'. It is one of the City's most famous and interesting townscapes. Although changes have occurred it still retains buildings of the fifteenth and sixteenth century. Still in existence is 'Stepcote Hill', the original thoroughfare into the City and the delightful fifteenth century church of St. Mary's Steps. It is shown in a rather delapidated condition in this record, but at one time was an area of considerable wealth due to the influence of rich merchants. In the early twentieth century it tended to house the poorer Exeter families.

29. The West Quarter supplied a great deal of labour for the nearby 'Shillhay' where numerous industries prospered. Mills, foundries, tanneries, coal depots, breweries, timber yards and warehouses, all used the area to conduct their business. This particular record shows a young woman at work in a munitions factory during the First World War. The exact location is not known. (Circa 1916.)

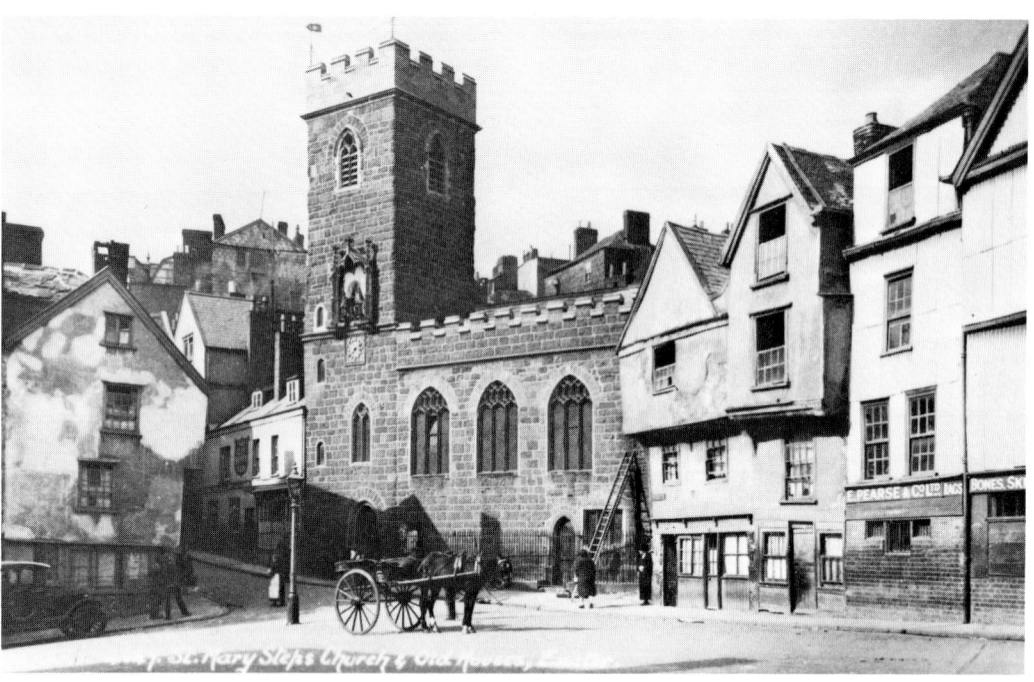

30. Shown left is a most interesting building that was demolished in the early 1940's. It was probably early fifteenth century. The empty site was to become the home of another building of approximately the same age that was resited in 1961. Exeter's famous 'House That Moved', as it is now called, was threatened with demolition and after much argument was placed on this corner site. It was moved on wheels and winched up from the corner of Frog Street to West Street. It was then carefully restored. It was the first time a house of such an age had been moved by this method and today is a tourist attraction. It was ironic that one building of equal interest should have been destroyed thus allowing another to take its place. The two buildings right of the Church were restored in the 1930's. Both are sixteenth century, but one is older than the other. To the far right is the business of 'E Pearse and Co', rag and bone merchants. They moved only recently. (1908.)

31. St. Mary's Steps Church has origins dating back to the twelfth century. Its name is derived from the steps of 'Stepcote Hill' which rise up beside the church. The building shown dates from the fifteenth century and contains within an excellent example of an early Norman font. The small door in the South wall leads into a room which was originally the 'Porters House' who was in charge of the West Gate. His job was to take tolls from visitors who entered the City.

32. The tower of St. Mary's Steps Church contains one of the most unusual and unique clocks in England. Dated circa 1656, the dial is decorated with reliefs depicting the four seasons. Above it are three figures within an alcove, of which the central character is thought to be Henry VIII. When the clock strikes the hour he bends forward on each stroke. The two javelin men on either side hold small hammers and strike the bells beneath them on the quarter hours. The clock was restored in 1982 and can still be seen in its original setting. The clock nicknamed 'Matthew the Miller' takes its name from a local miller who lived nearby. So punctual was the miller that the neighbourhood timed their day by his movements. On his death the clock was named after him as a gesture by the local people.

33. Stepcote Hill was once the main thoroughfare leading into the City, via the West Gate. This delightful street, much loved by artists and a unique feature, can still be seen today. The timber framed building on the left under went substantial restoration at a later date, but is shown here in poor condition. The properties seen on the other side of the street, at the junction of Ewings Lane, Edmund Street and West Street, were demolished in the early 1960's to allow the construction of a new inner by-pass.

34. At the turn of the century it would have been a normal sight to see children playing on Stepcote Hill. The outside steps were used for pedestrians, but the centre cobbled section was originally intended to be used by pack horses which brought goods into the City. In the 1930's changes were to take place that swept away many buildings in the West Quarter, the occupants being rehoused in other areas. For many years the area had been neglected and what was originally a townscape of rich merchants houses turned towards slum conditions. Recently the area has undergone improvements and once again life has been brought back to this ancient vicinity.

35. One of the most interesting features that was to be seen when entering Exeter, via Fore Street, was the clock of St. John's Church. Supported by a decorated bracket the clock overhung the pavement above the heads of passers by. In the past it has been described as 'a warm and comforting face that greeted you as you entered the City'. It had been nicknamed the 'Moon of Fore Street'. Number 110 Fore Street was one of two properties belonging to 'Walter Otton' the iron monger. In 1890 'Otton's' held the sole agency for 'Lancashire Patent Belting' acknowledged to be the finest of its type. It was 'unaffected by heat, water, steam, acid, runs true and steady and will do more work at less cost than single'! Otton's were the largest stockists of sheet and bar iron, as well as steel. (1905.)

36. This record gives some indication as to the steepness of Fore Street and the problems which the early horse drawn traffic had to overcome. To the left is St. John's Church and to the right is the entrance to Mint Lane which leads to St. Nicholas' Priory. St. John's Church was partly demolished in 1937 leaving only the tower to show its existence. This remnant stood for another twenty years and was finally demolished in 1957.

EXETER, ST. NICHOLAS PRIORY. WESTERN FRONT.

37. St. Nicholas' Priory is today used as local museum and displays within many interesting artifacts. Its foundation is traced back to the eleventh century and various periods of architecture can be seen throughout its structure. Only part of the original building exists today. Off the main route this ancient ecclesiastical building is often overlooked by visitors. Its magnificent fifteenth century guest hall is certainly worthy of inspection. A great deal of work has been put into restoring the building which was at one time used as a private dwelling.

38. One of the finest architectural features of the Priory is its early Norman undercroft.

39. In the grounds of the Priory stands the remains of a large Celtic shaft. It is thought to date from the eighth century and before arriving at the Priory stood at the corner of Gandy Street and High Street. Half of its length was sunken in the ground and was used to prevent damage occurring to number 229 High Street. Often carts would hit the side wall as they went to and fro. (Considerable wear can be seen on the edge of the stone.) It had remained on this corner for one hundred and thirty years when it was removed to the site shown. It was originally found when Exe Bridge was demolished in 1778. It was later purchased by the owner of the High Street premises.

40. Allhallows Church, as shown in this postcard, was removed just after the Second World War. It had been a replacement for an early Saxon church that had stood on the City Wall near the West Gate. The ancient church had been removed in 1770 during the construction of New Bridge Street. The foundation stone of the above building was laid on 22nd September 1843. According to reports its structure had little of architectural interest. Its fate had been sealed pre-war and had been closed since 1938 when its furnishings had been removed. It was finally demolished in 1950 amid complaints that it could have been used for a local hall, of which there was a shortage.

41. Built into the City Wall, above the Lower cemetery in Exe Street, is the Catacombs. Designed to create more space for burying the dead, the structure has hardly been used for the purpose intended. At one time access could be obtained to view the interior, but today the gate is firmly locked. It is onfortunate that this curiosity, which is more commonly seen abroad, cannot be made more visible for tourists. Today it is in a bad state of repair and the cemetery is sadly neglected. The Catacombs were built in 1835. (1905.)

42. The Mint Wesleyan Chapel, designed by methodist architect William Jenkins, built by John Brown, was opened in 1813. The site in Fore Street was previously that of the 'Arion Meeting House' which by 1810 had fallen into disuse. The Chapel bore the date 1812 but was finished in 1813. On March 25th of that year Joseph Entwistle (President Methodist Conference) and Reverend William Henshaw of Plymouth Dock preached to immense crowds assembled for the opening. It was said 'The Lord was powerfully present'. Singing was led by fiddles, flutes and a few singers and lighting was candles and oil lamps. The front portico was later added in 1815. For eighty-two years entrance to the Chapel was from Mint Lane or St. Olave's Square, the front being a burial ground up until 1867. This building has been demolished and replaced with a modern structure.

EXETER

43. The early eleventh century church of St. Olave's can still be seen today at the top of Fore Street, but the majority of buildings shown no longer exist. Almost opposite the church at the period shown was the premises of 'Henry Turner Furnishings and General Drapery'. A well known company in Exeter, 'Henry Turner' had two other properties in New Bridge Street. Every item for the home was available from his stores. He specialised in Dress and Mantle making and also millinery. Workshops carried out customers orders under specialist supervision. The results achieved a high degree of excellence 'Which redound equally to the satisfaction of customers and to the credit of the house'. The covered wagon shown was probably 'Turner's' as they did own such a vehicle which was used for delivery around the City.

44. The most prominent feature of this still surviving early thirteenth century church is its fine Norman arches from which it derives its name, St. Mary Arches. It was first recorded in the year 1222. The church attained a high civic importance which is borne out by the number of impressive monuments and wall plaques found within. Unfortunately the church completely lost its beautiful barrel roof as a result of enemy action during the last war. However it was restored in the 1950's thanks to a wooden barge that was dismantled at Topsham. Its substantial wooden timbers replaced the ancient beams that had been lost. (Circa 1910.)

45. This aerial view of the South Street area of the City (1925) is particularly interesting as it records many buildings that have long since been destroyed. The centre of the photo shows Holloway Street joining South Street and at this junction Magdalen Street connecting from the middle right. Bottom left shows Friars Walk leading to Friars Gate. Above this area is seen 'Folletts Building', a three storey tenement block, standing in Mermaids Yard. It housed the poorer working families. In the centre, top, is the lower market, blitzed during the war and later demolished. Top, far right, is the spire of St. Mary Majors Church which stood outside the West Front of the Cathedral.

46. One of the most attractive groups of buildings that Exeter possesses is 'Wynards Almshouses' in Magdalen Road, opposite the Eye Infirmary. Founded in 1430 as a charity, the group contains twelve cottages and a chapel. All the buildings are constructed around a central cobbled courtyard complete with a well beside which grows an evergreen oak tree. It is a most charming setting and in recent years has been subject to a great deal of restoration. It has been converted for use as offices for charities and other organisations. Originally it was intended to house twelve old men over sixty with their wives. Its last resident, a well known character, possessed an enormous white beard. He regularly appeared as father Christmas in a local store and children were amazed when the long white whiskers couldn't be pulled off! The little chapel contained carved oak stalls with the name of each occupant inscribed upon them. It was a custom for a service to be held annually attended by the Mayor and the corporation.

47. The Royal Devon and Exeter Hospital was opened in 1742. The three storeyed red brick front was completed in 1758, the pediment being added in 1772. A later edition was the present front door which was constructed in 1859 to give a grander entrance to the building. The photo shows the top of the cupola, a delightful feature dating from 1742. The railings, found on many buildings around Exeter, were placed on the frontage in 1831. The Royal Devon and Exeter Hospital (no longer a hospital) was one of the earliest hospitals in the country. As the postcard shows comfort must have been the first priority according to an inmate! In recent years severe damage was caused by a fire which severely gutted the third storey and roof, all of which has now been restored. (1909.)

48. Patients enjoy festivities in Dean Clarke Ward in the Royal Devon and Exeter Hospital.

Deaf & Dumb Institution, Exeter.

S.A.Chandler's
Real Photo Series
05056

49. The Royal School for the Deaf, earlier known as 'The Deaf and Dumb Institution', was founded by Mrs. Hippisley Tuckfield in 1826. The original premises used by the school was a rented property in Alphington causeway in January 1827. The first purpose built structure was erected 'Upon a delightful elevation on Topsham Road just within the Tollgate', the site shown here. It was purchased in November 1827. The school proved highly successful much being due to the tenacity of its original founder. In 1897 the property was extended at a cost of £6,023 and could then accommodate eighty-six boarders. Further extensions were carried out from 1947 onwards and by 1969 all the previous structures erected between 1826 and 1908 had been demolished and replaced with new. Today the site houses a sophisticated complex tailored to the needs of the deaf and without doubt is one of the finest establishments of its kind in England. (1915.)

Entrance to Barracks, Exeter.

50. The Higher Barracks, previously known as 'The Town Barracks', is possibly the only Cavalry Regiment Barracks left in the country. The original buildings, built of red brick with slate roofs, are dating from 1792. Further extensions took place in 1867. The design of the buildings reflected upon the importance which was placed on the horse, the officers being housed immediately above the stables. Today the barracks are used for Pay Offices, cadet training and general administration. The entrance is shown guarded both by man and machine. Recruitment posters adorn each side of the entrance. (1910.)

51. Taken just before the entrance to Broadgate and the Cathedral Close, this postcard shows the High Street continuing in its original width up to the London Inn Square. The photograph is interesting in as much as it is difficult to assess from where it was taken? It is too far out to be taken from a window. It has been taken just outside the premises of 'Garton and King' the Iron Mongers, Hot Water and Hydraulic Engineers. Although the shop front was of average proportions, it extended back to Waterbeer Street where they had a foundry. It was a very important business within the City for manufacturing all types of iron-mongery.

Guild Hall, Exeter.

52. A typical postcard which was on sale at the turn of the century showing the High Street and Guildhall. Use of the oval and painted wooden frames were a fairly popular feature. (Circa 1910.)

53. This early view of the High Street shows the street without tram lines. Trams started in Exeter around 1880 and were horse drawn. They were followed by electric trams after 1900. Clearly shown are the shop canopies which were supported by poles whose bases were inserted into holes in the kerb stones. The 'Turk's Head' public house, next to the Guildhall, is shown with a plain frontage and a lamp which advertised 'Alsopps Ales'. At a later date the 'Public Benefit Boot Company' and its neighbours were to disappear and replaced with a modern structure.

54. The 'Turk's Head' public house adjacent to the Guildhall has now aquired its new frontage, which is much grander than the former. Above the man, stood at the handcart outside, can be seen the carving of a 'Turks Head' from which the pub takes its name. The first floor window was removed and a glass and wooden screen inserted. The first floor room must have been completely removed. Such alterations clearly improved a previously darker interior. Charles Dickens is known to have been a frequent visitor to this ancient hostelry and his character 'The Fat Boy' in 'Pickwick' was said to have been found in the 'Turk's Head'. The new buildings on the corner of Goldsmith Street are now occupied by 'Samuels' the jewellers. Shops from this corner to Queen Street were to become part of the 'Waltons' complex. 'Knapmans the Drapers' are seen on the corner of Goldsmith Street, later to become 'Horne Bros.' and today 'Milletts' menswear and camping.

55. 1903 was to be the year in which the first tram lines were laid to take electric trams. A previous attempt using horse drawn vehicles had proved unsuccessful. In May 1897 a new route was opened which went from the Guildhall to Pennsylvania via Sidwell Street, Old Tiverton Road and Union Road. The route obviously proved too much for horse drawn trams as it was eventually abandoned.

OPENING OF EXETER ELECTRIC TRAMWAYS, APRIL 4TH, 1905.
Published by W. Chudley & Son, Exeter.

The Best Morning Paper for visitors to this district is the "Western Daily Mercury."

56. The opening of the tramways on April 4th, 1905. The vehicles are gathered outside the Guildhall and await the arrival of Mayor E.C. Perry, the first mayor to drive the new trams.

57. Exeter's Guildhall is the oldest municipal building in the country. Its first records date back to 1154 but its history is suspected to extend back much further. Great significance is given to the records stored within this building as they prove that Exeter has the longest unbroken written history of any City in the Kingdom. The impressive Elizabethan portico, which straddles the High Street pavement, at one time sheltered the City stocks. Drunkards and 'Ladies of leisure' often paid for their crimes by being placed in the instrument. This caused great amusement for the passer-by and children would often jear at the recipient.

58. On entering the Guildhall the visitor can often overlook one of the finest ancient doors that is left in the City. Massive in proportions, this late sixteenth century door is three inches thick. Beautifully carved it has, as an integral part of its design, a wicket door in its centre to allow access without having to open the whole door. This was a safety feature in times gone by. The door is dated at the same period as the portico, 1593.

59. Contained securely within the Guildhall and available for the visitor to see is the priceless City Regalia. The 'Sergeants At Mace' will describe these treasures on request. Within this collection is the sword of King Edward IV which was given to the City in 1473. The Cap of Maintenance and sword of Henry VII, which is carried before the Mayor on all state occasions, is dated 1497. The ancient maces and chains of office are used by the Mayor and Sherriff. The City Seals are said to be the oldest municipal seals in the Kingdom and are dated 1175. (Circa 1910.)

60. The impressive interior of the Guildhall has no exact date of construction but is of mediaeval origin. The first floor of the building was no more than beaten earth, but it was paved in 1660. The Hall measures 63 feet by 25 feet and its main feature is the superb timber framed roof. The walls, panelled in wood, are decorated with carved mouldings. The gallery above the front entrance probably held the first juries and was constructed around 1564. Many fine paintings hang in the building, all being portraits of civic dignitaries and famous people. One of the most prominent paintings is the portrait of Princess Henrietta Maria, daughter of Charles I. She was born in Exeter in 1643. (1911.)

61. A runner passes in front of the Guildhall while taking part in 'The West Of England Marathon' race on April 3rd, 1909. A similar race is still held today which attracts enormous crowds of people who cheer on the struggling participants!

62. The premises shown to the right of the Guildhall was known as 'All one price shop'. Its frontage displayed three decorative lamps. Any item could be purchased from this establishment at the cost of 6d! Adjacent to the Guildhall on the left is seen 'Olivers Shoe Shop'. It also had lamps above the windows to illuminate their goods in the evenings.

63. This postcard clearly records the demolition of the 'Public Boot Company' and shows the scaffolding still erected around the corner of Goldsmith Street and High Street. The studs which adjoined the 'Boot Company' to the adjacent building are seen projecting from the wall. Allhallows Church, a diminutive structure which had long since been a feature of the corner, was demolished in 1906. Further work is being carried out opposite the Guildhall, wooden scaffolding being in position. (1906.)

64. A slightly later record shows that reconstruction had finished on the Goldsmith site and that the new corner premises were occupied by 'Samuels' the jewellers. This building and its neighbours were demolished in 1979 as part of the development plan carried out by 'Marks and Spencer' who now occupy this very substantial central City site. The adjacent buildings, numbers 206 and 207 High Street, were business premises of 'Knapmans the Drapers'. It was later to be taken over by 'Horne Brothers' the outfitters. In recent years the building was demolished and reconstructed in its original design, in concrete. To those who did not know the building before hand no difference would be noticed.

65. At this point in the High Street the photographer was standing outside the premises of 'J. Webber and Sons', number 51 High Street, who were iron mongers. The shop was known locally as 'The Exeter Tool Chest'. Every manner of iron-mongery was to be found within as well as requirements for the sporting enthusiast. Bats, balls, racquets, nets, poles, leg guards, gauntlets, stumps, gloves, etc. This popular business still has premises in the City but are now in Queen Street. In addition to 51 High Street, 'Webbers' also had premises in Goldsmith Street, but this was for heavy duty goods. Adjacent to the High Street shop was a short cut to the Cathedral Yard. A charming thoroughfare called 'Exchange Lane', it was unfortunately demolished in 1962. (1909.)

66. Of all the businesses in Exeter's High Street probably the most well known was 'Mr. J. Hinton Lake, Pharmaceutical Chemist', who occupied a central and historic building. Number 41 High Street, an Elizabethan house, is dated 1564 and is almost opposite the corner of Queen Street with High Street. The business was established in 1868 and closed in January 1970. For nearly a century local folk had purchased medical supplies, photographic materials and equipment from this well known store. It was for many years the foremost stockist of photographic equipment and Mr. Lake particularly enjoyed this side of his business. A darkroom was placed at the disposal of his customers without charge and advice was freely given. Today this historic and valuable building is undergoing major changes and it is not yet known whether the result will be an improvement or loss to the City's heritage.

67. In latter years this corner building was better known as part of the 'Waltons' complex. It was demolished in 1978. The dome, which was a feature of this building, was saved and incorporated into a new structure designed for Marks and Spencer. The junction of Queen Street with High Street was always a busy place and with two way traffic there was often hold ups and jams. The local police would often be on duty to ensure a smooth flow of traffic. The officers who performed their duty regularly at this junction often received nicknames from the general public.

68. The façade seen left and occupied at this time by 'Boots' the chemist was constructed around 1850. It stretched from High Street to the corner of Little Queen Street. At one time graceful city houses, the whole structure was removed around 1969. It was unfortunate that this central site was to be built upon in a style that was totally lacking in sympathy with its surroundings and has been classified as one of Exeter's mistakes from an architectural point of view.

High Street, Exeter.

69. Pre-war the width of High Street remained the same from the corner of South Street to the London Inn Square and is faithfully captured in this record. Owing to the devastation that occurred in the Second World War, and to demolition, most of the upper High Street properties were swept away. The street was widened and new buildings erected. The major changes that took place was to change the character of the central area of the City and seemed to take little account of its historical aspects. The modern centre was unfortunately to be much the same as many other Cities who were built upon just after the war. Much more could have been retained and integrated into a more acceptable scheme for the City. Local decisions removed major portions of the City and replaced the whole with drab constructions. On the right is the entrance to St. Martin's Lane.

70. Taking the turning into St. Martin's Lane, past the famous 'Ship Inn', a drinking place of Sir Francis Drake, the visitor arrives at the Cathedral Yard. This corner of Exeter is one of its most famous architectural landscapes. To the left is shown the 'Exeter Bank', which is now part of 'The Royal Clarence Hotel'. It has recently been opened on the ground floor as a charming restaurant. Opposite, on the corner of Catherine Street, is the ancient church of Saint Martin. It was dedicated in 1065. The tower dates from 1675. The church contains some interesting mural monuments and also boasts a unique font. Exeter's most famous house, called 'Mols Coffee House', is next door. The railings shown around the 'Green' have long since been removed.

71. The famous Elizabethan house known as 'Mols Coffee House' dates from 1596. At one time owned by an Italian, 'Mr. Mol', the house became famous for its coffee and many famous people were entertained within. This practice continued until 1829 when it was taken over as an art gallery. The first floor room is called 'The Oak Room' and is beautifully panelled. Around the room are forty-six coats of arms reflecting upon the days of 'The Great Armada'. It is said discussions took place at 'Mols' relating to the planning of the battle. Many 'knights of the Garter' appear on the crests, the most famous being Sir Francis Drake and Sir Walter Raleigh. The ceiling, in the shape of a star, is said to be unique. For one hundred and fifty years the premises were known as 'Worths Art Gallery', but in 1982 changed to a jewellery business.

72. The Hooker Memorial stands on the Cathedral Green opposite 'Mols Coffee House'. It was unveiled by the Bishop of Exeter in 1907. The memorial was a gift from descendants of Hooker. The statue, made from white pantelican marble upon a pedestal of Devonshire granite, was said to have cost one thousand guineas. Richard Hooker was born in 1583, educated at Exeter School and died in 1660. He was the author of Ecclesiastical Policy.

73. St. Mary Majors Church stood in front of the West Front of Exeter Cathedral, until it was demolished in 1971. Visitors often wondered why a relatively modern building should have been erected so close to the Cathedral. The reason was that the site on which the church had been built had its history going back long before the West Front was constructed. The building shown was constructed in 1886 and some of the stones in the building had belonged to the previous structure which had been demolished. The Victorian church had little of interest architecturally and in its latter years was little used. It was decided therefore that its removal would improve the general vista of the Cathedral and in particular expose the West Front further.

74. The interior of St. Mary Majors Church. After demolition of the church and examination of its foundations major archaeological roman remains came to light. Over a period of time a Roman bath house was uncovered and clarified beyond all doubt the importance of Exeter as a Roman garrison. Being such a substantial find it was hoped that it could have been preserved under a roof and made to be a tourist attraction. However the cost of the roof was never found and the whole site was later filled in.

75. Due to the removal of the gutted Globe Hotel, after the Second World War, the photographer has been given a unique opportunity to record a corner of the Cathedral Close. In the foreground stands a group of three sixteenth century houses known as 'The Gables', at one time utilised by craftsmen attached to the Cathedral. Two statues situated on the frontage of the nearest property still reflect upon the masons art. Today these buildings are used by solicitors and a gift shop. St. Mary Majors Church obscures the front of the Cathedral. At this time the Great West window still retained its bomb blast screen. The early ancient stained glass had been removed previous to its erection. Nearly all the Cathedral windows sustained war damage. (Circa 1948.)

Exeter Cathedral, West Front.

76. Exeter's magnificent cathedral has a history which spans over a thousand years and is known as 'The Jewel of the West'. This view of the West Front is perhaps the best known to visitors. The Western screen was constructed between 1370-1394 and consists of three rows of statues each being set in a niche. Each statue represents an angel, saint, apostle, etc. The statue surmounting the gable is that of Saint Peter, patron saint of the Cathedral. The West Front underwent some restoration at the turn of the century and today is still the subject of a major programme to retain it for future generations. The Cathedral suffered from damage by smoke owing to the dropping of incendiaries during the war, but in recent years has gradually been cleaned.

77. An attractive view of the Norman South Tower and the entrance to the Bishops Palace. The South Tower holds the heaviest peal of bells in England and are unmatched for their quality of tone. The massive Grandisson bell cast in 1727 weighs 10,522 lbs. In 1901 the bells were rehung as the method of ringing was antiquated. A new cage was constructed which allowed the ringer to utilise the minimum amount of effort to perform his task. The chiming gear enabling this to take place was invented by Reverend H.T. Ellacombe, Rector of Clyst St. George. (1912.)

78. The great fourteenth century window undergoes restoration at the turn of the century. On 1st July 1904 restoration work started and valuable ancient stained glass was removed. The work cost around two thousand guineas and was subscribed to by eleven hundred individuals as a memorial to Archbishop Temple, a former Bishop of Exeter. The stone work was carried out by Messrs. Luscombe of Exeter, the architect Mr. Bodley R.A. and the artists, Burlisson and Grylls of London.

Bishop's Palace, Exeter.

79. It is unfortunate that today the rear of the Cathedral and the Bishops Palace cannot be viewed from the gardens, as it presents one of the loveliest views of this fine building. At one time the general public were allowed access to the gardens, but some years ago this privilege was stopped. The Palace, which adjoins the Cathedral on the south side, was started in 1381. It underwent considerable restoration between 1837 and 1869. Within the building is an exceptionally fine armorial mantle piece known as 'The Courtenay Mantlepiece'. This superb mediaeval masterpiece stands twelve feet high and eight feet wide. It is enriched with coats of arms and carvings which reflect upon the history of the Courtenay family. During the restoration of the palace an ancient window was removed from a house by the Globe Hotel and inserted into the building.

80. The south east view taken from the Bishops garden clearly shows the flying buttresses which supports the longest Gothic roof in Europe. The total length of this excellent example of Gothic architecture, and the most notable feature of its interior, is 409 feet. To the bottom left is seen the Chapel of St. Mary which at one time was a chantry.

81. The east window, found beyond the Choir, is early perpendicular in style and dates from the fourteenth century. The ancient stained glass is very fine and depicts at the bottom shields of early Bishops and benefactors and above that of numerous saints. Provision of this magnificent work is given to Henry De Blakeborne, a canon of the church, who offered one hundred marks for its construction in 1839. The glazier, a Mr. Robert Lyen, was paid twenty pence for fitting every foot of new glass and for refitting the old three shillings and four pence per week.

82. There are few examples of fine early doors left in the City but one which avoided the ravages of time, including war damage, is that which is found at number 10 The Close. A massive studded door dating between 1597 and 1621, it leads into the courtyard of the Quadrangle. Above the door, on the exterior of the building, can be seen the Arms of Bishop Cotton dating from the reign of James I. A delightful wicket gate allows access for pedestrians.

THE OLD COURTYARD, CATHEDRAL CLOSE, EXETER

83. Passing through an arched passageway at Number 10 The Close, the visitor can immediately step back into the past. Better known as 'The Quadrangle', this courtyard is full of all the old world charm. In season an old twisted wysteria comes into bloom and its clusters of blue blossoms add further to the beauty of this tranquil spot. Originally the buildings belonged to a religious community. Contained within is a chapel and a refectory. A dormitory can also be traced. The house has a ceiling upon which is carved the Arms of Courtenay, Hake, Bishops, Fox, Lacy, Oldham, and Lady Margaret Beaufort, his Patroness.

4290. EXETER CATHEDRAL FROM CANON NAYLORS BRIDGE.

84. An unusual view looking towards the rear of the Cathedral which has been taken underneath the small iron footbridge which spans a gap in the City Wall. The bridge was erected by Mr. Burnett Patch in 1813 when he was Mayor of Exeter. The lane joins the Cathedral Close to Southernhay.

85. The late seventeenth century Globe Hotel stood in the corner of the Cathedral Yard opposite the West Front of the Cathedral. Having been established for many years, it was one of the City's foremost hotels. Often advertisements would appear in City Guides and read as follows: *Old Established family and commercial Hotel, centre of City, Tudor period oak panneled smoke lounge, away from all noise and traffic facing west front of Cathedral, electric light, good cuisine, private standing room for cars.* Unfortunately this fine Hotel was gutted by fire during the last war and could not be saved. Its remaining shell was demolished.

THE DEANERY, EXETER.   HH 953

86. Opposite the Cathedral Cloisters, behind a wall, can still be seen the Deanery. The building, which has some splendid rooms, has often been visited by royalty. The history of The Deans of Exeter is a long one which stretches back to 1225 when Serlo was made the first Dean of Exeter. Originally the Deanery adjoined what was known as 'Kalendarhay', a group of houses used by vicars. Erected in the late fourteenth century, the site consisted of houses on the north and south side of a lane with a common hall at the west end. A kitchen backed onto South Street. For a time the houses were known as 'Cook Row'. By the mid-nineteenth century many of the buildings were unused and eventually the houses on the south side were removed and the site ended up as part of the Deanery garden. The remaining houses were later demolished enabling St. Mary Majors Church to be built. The spire of the church is seen behind the Deanery.

Exeter Cathedral Close Elizabethan House.

87. Pre-war this fine house could be found in the north east corner of 'The Close' attached to the 'Headmasters House' of the Cathedral School. It was known as 'The town house of the Bishops of Buckfastleigh' who occasionally leased the property. Its origins could be traced back to the early fifteenth century, but the house shown was apparently constructed around the late sixteenth century. On its façade is seen a sun dial with the bust of 'Good Queen Bess' over the porch. The building was occupied by a number of wealthy families over the centuries, but it was finally purchased by the Dean and Chapter in 1847. The shield over the door is that of the Rodd family and reads: 'Vincit Veritas'. An interior room also bore coats of arms including the royal coat of arms.

88. A general view of the centre of High Street looking towards the junction of Queen Street with High Street. On the left corner can be seen the premises of 'Colsons', one of the most notable stores in the city at this time. On the right is 'Ross, the tailors and outfitters'. One of his adverts is shown on the wall.

89. A pre-war police parade (date unknown) passes by some of the City's most prestigious historical buildings. In the centre of the photograph, underneath the dome of a street lamp, is number 229 High Street. This ancient property was demolished in 1930 and replaced with a very poor substitute. The original building shown here had splendid carvings and Jacobean panneling around its rooms. Its interior was ripped out and exported to America. It was at the corner of this building that a Celtic cross had been placed, which is now found in St. Nicholas' Priory. The Replacement structure for 229 High Street is an unsympathetic building having inserted into its design windows taken from ancient property in North Street. In latter years the premises were well known as 'Lyons' and today is a boutique.

90. Of all the businesses in Exeter at the turn of the century 'Ross the tailors and outfitters' was probably one of the best known. The premises was 227 High Street, shown right. This seventeenth century building is still classified as one of the finest examples in the City. Sadly only the façades exist today and even these have been unsatisfactorily integrated with modern architecture. Originally both of the properties shown would have been owned by wealthy merchants. At this time 226 was a local newspaper office and 227 'Ross'. It was said that in olden days bulls were baited opposite these properties and that the residents watched from the balconies! 'J & G Ross' attained the highest reputation in their field. They were said to hold the largest stocks available, 'of which they are able to recommend on the grounds of durability and general wearing excellence'. They specialised in shirt making, hosiery, gloves, hats and outfits. (Circa 1911.)

91. This special event was recorded outside of 'Colsons', the well known High Street store (now Dingles). Mayor E.C. Perry is seen driving the first electric tram in 1905. He also drove the last tram in 1931.

J. R. Browning, Photo. Exeter. Copyright.

EXETER ELECTRIC TRAM,
Decorated Car Driven by the Mayor E. C. Perry. Esq. April 4th 1905

92. An interesting souvenir postcard from Exeter which has a distinct lack of professionalism! It appears to have been done by hand and some of the views are lacking in description. Bottom left, entrance to Bampfylde House, middle 'Mols Coffee House', right 'Chevalier Inn' Fore Street, (incorrectly titled), top left '226/227 High Street', middle 'The Guildhall', right 'Doorway to the Quadrangle', centre 'Interior courtyard of the Quadrangle' (not named).

93. Queen Street, being the main road into the City from the north, has always attracted a good deal of traffic. Many people came in from the country to sell their goods in the market, seen half way along the street on the left. The Higher Market in Queen Street was constructed to clear away the street markets which often caused congestion. The new building was opened on 24th July 1838. It was closed 124 years later in 1962. This record shows that the corner premises was at this time occupied by 'Wheatons' the printers.

94. Dominating the top of some fine buildings in Queen Street can be seen (1907) the statue of 'Queen Victoria', from which the street obtains its name. Previously it had been known as Higher Market Street. The statue was erected by George Ferris, owner of the properties, in 1848 for the birthday of Queen Victoria. The statue remained insitu for one hundred and thirty years when it was taken down before the buildings were demolished. It was decided to retain the statue and a replica was made. The façades of the building were also reconstructed in concrete.

Exeter. Queen Street, looking West   Valentines Series 51622

95. On the corner of Upper Paul Street and Queen Street (right) is seen the premises of 'St. Anne's Well Brewery', the Wine and Spirit Merchants. The company had occupied the site from around 1890 and continued business for eighty years. Shown to the left is the turning into Paul Street and on the corner the Museum Hotel which was demolished around 1926. The site was to become in 1932 the City's Information Bureau, a timber framed building which has only recently disappeared as part of a road improvement plan. Adjacent to the Bureau was the Coach Station and Car Park. It was opened in 1931 and continues to be used for car parking space. (1911.)

96. Exeter Museum, known correctly as 'The Royal Albert Memorial Museum', was dedicated to the Prince Consort and founded in 1865. The Memorial building contains a museum, art gallery, and School of Art. Over the years the museum has aquired numerous collections of significance. The Peel and Bradshaw collection of Great Game animals, hunting trophies from Sir Samuel Baker, The Perhouse collection of Birds, The Linter collection of land shells of the world, The Champerdowne collection of British fossils, a superb tiger shot by George V in 1913 and presented in the same year, The Dennet collection of African fetish figures, The Peard collection of Esquimaux implements and carvings, The Dewdney collection of North American Indian Relics, etc. The Museum houses a substantial collection of paintings, etchings and drawings and although changes have occurred within the building, it remains one of the finest in England. (1907.)

97. Early advertisements relating to the Rougemont Hotel display a reproduction of a stained glass window that can be found on the premises. It depicts scene two, Act four of Richard III and shows the King surrounded by his noblemen and soldiers. A large gateway stands behind and a quotation underneath reads: *When last I was at Exeter, the Mayor in courtesy show'd me the castle and called it 'Rougemont' at which name I started, because a Bard of Ireland told me once I should not live long after I saw Richmond.* The Hotel offered one hundred rooms and suites, electric light and lift, London band and dancing during Winter, Trams met by appointment, garage with inspection pit. The largest and only modern Hotel in Exeter.

98. The Clock Tower, found at the junction of Queen Street and New North Road, replaced a lesser structure known as 'The Quadrant'. It was a watering place for horses that passed in and out of the City by the northerly route. The elegant Clock Tower was erected in 1897 and was opened in 1898 by Mrs. Miles in memory of her husband. He was a well known philanthropist and animal lover. The opening ceremony was carried out by Mrs. Miles, who arrived in a carriage drawn by two magnificent grey horses. These were the first animals to drink from the fountain. The structure has often been criticised for its position and attempts have been made to remove it. However it still stands today, but no longer used for its original purpose.

Exeter's First
Electric Tram
Driven by the
Mayor.
(E. C. Perry, Esq.)
Tuesday
April 4th 1905.

99. A memorable occasion as the Mayor E.C. Perry Esq. drives the first electrically operated tram on Tuesday 4th April 1905. The tram has just passed the Clock Tower and stands outside the 'Osborne Hotel', on its way to St. David's Station. The advert on the tram relates to 'Green and Sons Costumiers and Milliners' of 25 and 26 High Street. Situated next to St. Stephen's Bow, 'Greens' premises contained the famous 'Apollo' ceiling, which could be inspected by visitors. This superb decorated plaster ceiling was found in a room formerly used as a banquetting hall for judges on circuit. It was dated 1695. The room was used by 'Greens' to display furs and mantles.

100. At the junction of Hele Road and New North Road stands the equestrian statue of Redvers Buller, a famous West Country Soldier. His numerous battles won him many honours, much of his time being spent in Africa, China, Canada and South Africa. An avid farmer Redvers Buller lived at 'Downes' near Crediton. He attained a high reputation for the quality of his stock. In particular he was well known for the excellence of his horses, for which he had great admiration. He died in 1901 and statues were erected to his memory in Plymouth and Exeter. The statue in Exeter was unveiled by the Lord Lieutenant of Devon, Viscount Ebrington, on 6th September 1905. (1906.)

101. The unveiling of Buller's statue on 6th September 1905.

102. Buller's favourite horse followed the gun carriage at the funeral.

ST. DAVIDS STATION, EXETER

103. St. David's Station was opened on 1st May 1844. The Director 'Special' left Paddington, London at 7.30 a.m., to attend the opening ceremony and arrived at St. David's at 12.45 p.m. Initially the station consisted of two buildings in drabesque style, but in 1862 a new station was started and duly opened in July 1864. The new structure consisted of four platforms, an ornamental frontage and a partly glazed roof 132 feet wide and 363 feet long. It was 43 feet above rail level and was claimed to be 'A wonder of the Age'. A branch line was opened to the Basin for the transportation of goods on 17th June 1867. The station was rebuilt again in the years 1911-1914 with the old frontage being retained. In this record a tram is shown waiting outside the station entrance. (1907.)

104. St. Michael's Church stands on an area known as Mount Dinham, a cliff top site which overlooks the River Exe. The church's high tower is one of the City's most conspicuous sights. From base to top the tower rises up over 230 feet. 'Saint Michael's and All Angels' Church was erected in 1868 and consecrated on the 30th September. Built in Gothic style, its construction was carried out in limestone. Adjacent to the church is a delightful group of 'Almshouses for deserving persons'. Mr. Dinham, who bought the ground, built twenty-four cottages himself and a further sixteen were added by contributors. The cottages arranged in groups have walkways with gardens and shrubs. In 1860 the Episcopal Charity School was moved to Mount Dinham, and after its construction, the remaining land was purchased by Mr. Dinham. The school is no longer used for its original purpose, but is now an annexe to the Exeter College of Art. It was founded by Bishop Blackall (1708-1716) and attained a high reputation as a secondary modern school.

105. In the centre of High Street stands the Church of St. Stephen's. Built around 1664, the building has embattlements which are typical of most of the City's ancient churches. The most famous feature of the building is not shown, it is a Bow, called St. Stephen's Bow. It extends to the left of the building and above it rests the Chancel. Walking underneath it you arrive in Catherine Street. Mentioned in the Domesday Book, this church has retained an interesting crypt which was rediscovered in 1826. The existence of the crypt could be traced back to 1658 when it was used as a stable. At this time the church was undergoing repairs and was completely rebuilt. The crypt however remained and was reopened nearly two hundred years later. There is no access to it today.

106. Built of Heavitree stone, the church of St. Lawrence stood in High Street until just after the Second World War. The building, seen right, was gutted by fire and later the shell demolished. The prominent south porch had a small alcove above the door in which was placed a figure of Elizabeth I. It is the only remnant of the church left today. The porch had been constructed from materials taken from a demolished conduit that stood at the top of High Street. The statue was also taken from this structure later being placed on the front of the church. This photo shows the tram lines, that were laid in 1903. The trams ran from the Guildhall to Pennsylvania. Shown on the left is the turning into Bedford Street with the Half Moon Hotel on the corner. (1909.)

DELLER'S
CAFÉ
. . .
EXETER

107. Dellers Café in Bedford Street was the most sumptuous of all premises in Exeter for eating and entertainment. The Grand entrance was in Bedford Street, but the building continued around into High Street. The ground floor was occupied by Lloyds Bank. The showpiece of the Café was its wonderful balconied interior decorated with reliefs. A Palm Court Orchestra played on the ground floor. Many functions took place in this fabulous building which was gutted by fire during the war. Although most of the external structure still stood it was demolished. Opened in 1916, Dellers was equipped with a ballroom and banquetting halls decorated to the highest standards and capable of handling the largest functions. The Café was never forgotten and unfortunately no building has ever replaced the splendid 'Dellers Café'.

Bedford Circus, Exeter.

108. Bedford Circus, an excellent example of Georgian architecture, was situated on the site where the main Post Office stands today. It consisted of elegantly constructed private houses and a chapel, the whole being centred around a large circular garden. A famous landmark in the City, Bedford Circus also suffered in the last war. A substantial portion remained and it was recommended that it should have been restored. The whole site was removed owing to a local decision. It was a most unfortunate error of judgement. A superb piece of the City's heritage was lost forever. Various businesses operated from the Circus including: Charles Ware Surveyors, Bedford Car Washing Agency, Cherry and Cherry Estate Agents and Henry Wykes photographer. In 1890 the 'Devonshire Baryta Chemical Company' had premises at number 15. Baryta, a mineral, was mined at Bridford and was found to have special qualities for paint production giving a more permanent and sun resistant product. (1903.)

109. Taken just at the turn of the century, (1904), this postcard shows, on the left, the turning into Castle Street from High Street. It is not often recorded. Opposite is the turning into Post Office Street. On the corner, on the left hand side, above the heads of pedestrians, hangs a cows head. This belonged to 'Havill and Sons' the butchers. The large building halfway up on the right was the Post Office. Note at this time there are no tram lines in High Street.

110. 'Castle Street College Hostel', now called 'Bradninch House', stands just outside the entrance to Rougemont Castle. The Norman Gatehouse is seen left. In 1902 a syndicate bought the premises called 'Vineyard' and turned the Georgian house into a hostel for 'Women students in training who lived outside the City'. The bedrooms became dormitories divided by serge curtains. A Common Room and Study was provided. The furnishings were austere. Miss Montgomery, the founder of the syndicate, acted as warden and ruled with an iron hand. The building was soon too small so 'Bradninch House' in Gandy Street was purchased to accommodate a further twenty students. The building was later demolished and the New College erected. New wings were added to 'Vineyard' to take a further seventy students. It was renamed 'Bradninch House'. The Hostel doors closed at 7 p.m. Religious exercises were received daily and the regime was taken without complaint.

Rougemont Castle, Exeter.

111. Turning into Castle Street from High Street and continuing one is confronted by the massive entrance to Rougemont Castle. The impressive Gatehouse Tower is the original early Norman tower which is sometimes confused with being Saxon. The modern entrance to the Castle, seen right, was constructed around 1770. The large doorway, shown left, leads to Rougemont Gardens, at this time a private garden. It was owned by Miss Outhwaite who allowed visitors to see the gardens, but only on Thursdays and by leaving their calling cards at the door! Rougemont Gardens was handed over to the City and were opened to the public on the 12th April 1912.

112. Taken from the Castle courtyard looking towards the main gate, the wall of the Porters Lodge is seen on the left. After problems with sanitation within the Castle in 1891, the Lodge was declared as being unfit for habitation and was demolished. Its replacement was built at the Queen Street entrance to Northernhay Gardens.

Topsham Barracks, Exeter.

113. The postcard claims that the photograph is that of Topsham Barracks but this is incorrect. It is the Court House within the Castle grounds and was built in 1774. The building has been for assizes and quarter sessions and today is maintained as a Crown Court. The two guns placed outside relate to the First World War. The central statue is that of Hugh Earl Fortescue, Lord Lieutenant of Devon. It was erected in 1863 and has since been moved to the side of the building.

Northernhay, Exeter.

114. Northernhay Gardens are the oldest public gardens in England being converted into a public walkway around the year 1612. Although severely damaged during the civil wars, they were restored fifty-two years later. These charming gardens, which overlook the green hills on the northern side of the City, has always been a favourite haunt for residents. Until recently the gardens boasted many fine elm trees which unfortunately have now been cut down. Placed around the gardens are also fine statues dedicated to Devon Worthies. John Dinham, founder of 'Mount Dinham Almshouses for Unfortunate tradesmen', and Sir Thomas Dyke Acland Bart, are works carried out by the sculptor C.B. Stephens. The superb bronze called 'The Deer Stalker' is by the same artist and wins great admiration. Shown in the centre of this photograph is the statue of the Late Earl of Iddesleigh, better known as 'Sir Stafford Northcote'. It was erected in 1887 after his death.

115. Coming from Rougemont Gardens into Northernhay one passes through an archway which pierces the City Wall. The first view into Northernhay is that of the War Memorial which was erected after the First World War. It is an extremely impressive work which was carried out by John Angel, a native of the City. It is credited to be one of the finest memorials in the country. Designed around a large granite plinth, the main figure is that of 'Victory' who is trampling the demon of Tyranny and Wrong. On each of the four sides of the memorial are life size bronzes depicting a soldier, sailor, prisoner of war and a nurse. (1923.)

116. An early view of Northernhay Gardens in full summer bloom. The statue of Sir Thomas Dyke Acland Bart was to be removed from the position shown and today stands beside the City Wall further down the gardens towards Queen Street. The site was to be used for the War Memorial which was commissioned after the First World War. The wall shown was also removed.

"There's no place like Home"
The County Prison. Exeter

117. An appropriate message on this postcard (1905), 'Theres no place like home', comes from the County Prison in New North Road. It possibly came from one of the inmates! The County Prison was built in 1853 and was designed by the architect John Hayward. The site was previously that of the 'Bridewell' which was built in 1810. The only remnants of this previous structure is the heavily rusticated and vermiculated stone gateway. Designed by George Money Penny, its design was suggested by the side doors of Burlington House, London. The first person to be executed at the new prison was George Sparks, who was dispatched in 1855.

118. To the right is shown the entrance to Northernhay Gardens as entered from Queen Street. The gardens had a reputation for its fine elm trees which shaded the visitor during the summer months. Alas there are few trees left today, probably because of Dutch Elm Disease which was prolific in the county some years ago. At the entrance gate stands the Porters Lodge, built in 1891. The original building had stood in the Castle courtyard. The road shown to the left leads down into Central Station which was completely rebuilt in 1933. The new structure was held as being an excellent example of what a modern station should be! It is little used today. The County Prison can be seen in the background.

119. One of Exeter's most reputable butchering establishments was that of 'Havill and Son' of number 5 High Street. The property, shown right, extended around the corner into Post Office Street. The open fronted shop had marble slabs to display the various meats. Carcasses would be hung up whole in the window. The company had been in existence for nearly one hundred years before this photograph was taken. The business dated back to 1800. Leaders in their field, 'Havill and Son' dealt with a great many trade matters and were often to be seen at markets and fairs buying high quality sheep and cattle. Only the most tender and wholesome of meat would be purchased. The Company also had another property in Heavitree and specialised in selling real Exmoor Down and Dartmoor Mutton. (Circa 1906.)

120. The large three storeyed building half way up High Street, on the right, was the new Post Office. It consisted of a spacious public office, sorting office, first floor telegraphic room, retiring rooms and sanitary offices for the telegraphist. A storeman and caretaker were on the third floor. The building was enlarged in 1932. This new structure was opened in 1885. The postal service had started in 1805 in a premise in front of the Cathedral where mail was delivered by an old woman. The service later moved to Gandy Street then Cathedral Yard and after to Post Office Street where four staff were employed and the Exwick mail arrived by donkey! The first purpose built building was Post Office Chambers in Queen Street. It was constructed from Portland stone and brick at a cost of £10,000. Shown on the left hand side of High Street, above the heads of passers-by, is the decorated sign of 'Prettys Hair Cutting Rooms', one of Exeter's high class tonsorial artists!

121. The arcade in High Street, better known as 'The East Gate Arcade', was built in 1882 and was one of the most fashionable places in which to shop before the last war. A glass covered structure with a beautifully decorated oval window which faced the visitor as they entered, the Arcade, with its suspended and bracketed wall lamps, had a charm of its own. The 'Arcade Photographic Company' had premises at number 6 and was well known for the quality of their work. Established in 1852 and occupying numbers 3 and 4 The Arcade, was the business of Miss Mapledoram. She specialised in 'Ladies and Gents Ready Made Linen and Outfitting'. An extensive stock was maintained. The shop front of number 3 displayed gentleman's goods and number 4 was used for ladies' and children's wear. Number 22 was occupied by 'R.H. Cummings Umbrella and Parasol Maker'. An umbrella was suspended from a bracket outside his shop. The entrance to the Arcade is seen left, decorated with flags and displaying an external clock.

122. Situated on the corner of Longbrook Street and New North Road, the Theatre Royal occupied a prime central site in the City. It was erected in 1886, but suffered a tragic fire on 5th September 1887. The previous Theatre, which had been in Bedford Street, also suffered the same fate. The fire of 1887 was responsible for the deaths of nearly two hundred people who couldn't get clear of the raging inferno. Some threw themselves off the outer balconies into the street, others were trampled to death, others suffocated in the choking smoke. The theatre was rebuilt in 1889 and because of legislation was the first theatre to have a safety curtain. It was hauled down by hand and weighed four and a half tons. Some of the most famous actors and actresses that this country has seen played at the Theatre Royal. Musicals, Plays, Music Hall, Operas, and every form of entertainment to be found in a prominent theatre, took place in this building. Classified as being one of the most historic theatres in the country, it was sadly demolished in 1962 due to lack of support. (1908.)

123. The gruesome fire of 1887 left the Theatre Royal a gutted ruin. The bodies of 186 people were recovered and laid out in the stables of the London Inn where they could be identified. The entrance to the stables are seen on the left opposite the Theatre. The New London Inn Hotel was a high class Hotel and had been visited by some very famous people, including Robert Louis Stevenson. Within the building was a charming covered cobbled courtyard decorated with palms and arm chairs so that the visitor could take his ease. Following the fire at the Theatre, an inquest stated that bad design and construction were the chief cause of the tragedy. People had been trapped in the narrow exits and had panicked. Bodies were found one on top of the other. Today the site of the Theatre has been taken over as an insurance company. The hut seen in New North Road was used by the local police.

R.M.S. TITANIC.

HIPPODROME, EXETER,

Week Commencing: —Nov. 25th,

124. Within the London Inn Square, to the left of the New London Inn, was the Royal Public Rooms. The site is now occupied by 'Boots' the chemists. Acquired by Mr. Fred Karno, the premises were turned into the Hippodrome Theatre. Equipped with a new stage, seating and redecorated, the Theatre played host to reknowned artists such as Marie Lloyd and Harry Tate. The stalls were reached by an underground passage! The Hippodrome was taken over and turned into the Plaza Cinema until it was blitzed during the Second World War. 'The loss of the Titanic' was a major spectacle presented at the Hippodrome and comprised of eight tableaux. It was the work of Charles and John Pooles. It consisted of: 1. The marine effect of the vessel leaving Southampton, 2. Cork Harbour, Titanic Outward Bound, 3. Mid Ocean, 4. The SS Touraine in the Icefield, 5. Approaching iceberg, 6. The great vessel sinking, 7. The arrival of Carpathian and rescuing of survivors, 8. The vision. Unique mechanical and electrical effects, special music and the story was described in a thrilling manner!

125. Occupying a substantial site on the corner of Paris Street, Sidwell Street and Southernhay, the Bude Hotel was one of the oldest coaching houses in the City. It could be traced to 1358. In 1668 it was known as 'The London Inn' and was a major coaching establishment. In 1763 reaching London took two days by stage coach. It was later reduced to fifteen hours. It was said three hundred horses were kept at the Inn. Royal visitors included The Duke of York 1763, the Duke of Gloucester 1781, the Prince of Wales (after George IV) in 1788. King George III arrived with the Duke of York at a later date. Sadler, the pioneer of ballooning, also resided complete with balloon! The Hotel covered a quarter of an acre, but its corner site was regarded as a traffic hazard. The building was offered for sale in 1927 and 1930. It was bought by the council in 1933 as part of a road improvement plan. The frontage was demolished and the remainder sold to L.H. Fearis (Grocers) for £18,000. The building was then completely demolished and replaced by a modern structure. (1911.)

In Affectionate Remembrance of

"They did their work; their day is done."

"Ring out the old, ring in the new."

The EXETER HORSE TRAMS,
Which succumbed to an Electric Shock, April 4th, 1905.

126. The last of the horse drawn trams recorded in Sidwell Street. The Bude Hotel is seen to the right on the corner of Paris Street.

St. Luke's Training College, Exeter.

127. The Exeter Diocesan Training College is today simply known as 'St. Luke's College'. Its function is for training school masters. The foundation stone was laid on the 19th May 1853. It was the first public training school in the country and was officially opened on 18th October 1854. The chapel, shown to the right, was built in 1863 and was enlarged in 1911. The main building and hostels stand in seven acres of ground and over the years substantial expansion of the College has taken place. All denominations are catered for. St. Luke's College has achieved a high reputation, particularly in the field of physical education. (1912.)

SAINT LUKE'S COLLEGE. EXETER.   NORTH FRONT.

128. The north view of St. Luke's College with a patriotic flag flying in the front entrance. The trees in the foreground have been an after thought by the printers who have painted them in.

Fore Street – Heavitree (looking up)

129. One mile from the Guildhall can be found the suburb of Heavitree which extends east and north of the City. The route for trams was extended in to Heavitree and the first electric tram arrived there on 4th April 1905. Today Heavitree still retains its character although almost integrated with the City. The lamp-post, shown right, bears the following inscription: 'Presented to his native parish by J.R. Nethercott Esq JP, Chairman of the Council 1911-1912.' To the right is North Street and inserted into the wall opposite at this junction with Fore Street is a stone tablet which records that 'the thoroughfare was widened in 1910 by Heavitree Urban Council'. The United Reform Church in Fore Street has two foundation stones, one on each side of the entrance. One reads: 'To the Glory of God, Miss Ellen Stewart Williams of Exeter, September 29th 1902'. The other stone reads: 'Richard Williams Harold Row, Fred Commins, Arch, Stephens and Sons Builders.'

130. Heavitree Bridge was at one time to be found at the junction of Rifford Road and Honiton Road at the bottom of East Wonford Hill. There are few signs to show the existence of this site today. Even the stream which flowed under the bridge cannot be seen. To the left is recorded the charming houses that stood on East Wonford Hill. Built in the early eighteenth century, both of the houses were demolished in 1966. Further along the valley (to the left) can be found the ruin of St. Loyes Chapel, originally known as St. Eligius, but no trace will be found of the almshouses which were in close proximity to the building.

131. Sidwell Street at the turn of the century was one of Exeter's busiest streets and contained a wealth of different trades. Many of these businesses occupied interesting and historic buildings. Buildings shown on the right hand side of the street in this record were to sustain severe damage during the war and also some premises on the left. However in the 1960's what buildings of character were left were unfortunately demolished only to be replaced with some cold modern architecture. Very little exists of the pre-war street today. In this photograph the property shown second left was that of 'John Frost' Tea and Grocery Dealer. It was number 155 Sidwell Street. Established around 1845, the premises were known as 'St. Sidwells Tea Warehouse'. Mr. Frost was well known for the quality and purity of his teas. Every manner of product was stocked that was affiliated to the grocery trade including coffee imported from the West Indies. Sugar, Spices, Sago, Rice, Fruits, Sauces, Pickles, Salmon, Bacon, Cumberland Ham, and products from the American markets were sold.

132. At the junction of York Road and Sidwell Street stands the popular public house called 'The Duke of York'. It has recently been completely refurbished in Victorian style complete with working gas lamps. An advertisement shown on the exterior wall in this record refers to 'William Rouch Veterinary Surgeon'. Behind the pub is seen the roof of the 'New Wesleyan Church'. It was opened on May 3rd, 1905. It was described as 'A hansome and unique edifice which is the first building in England to be constructed on the Cottancin System of steel, cored brick and steel covered cement concrete'. Its gallery, unsupported by any columns, is 60 feet square and gives an uninterrupted view of all 803 seats. The ground floor seats 528, the gallery 245 and the choir 30. The building rises 85 feet from pavement to the finial of the cupola. The foundation stone was laid December 3rd, 1902 and the building cost £9,600.

133. The Girls Middle School (known as Bishop Blackall) was founded by Bishop Blackall in 1709 as a Trust. The school was approved under the 'Endowed Schools Act' (1869) in 1875. Standing on Pennsylvania Hill, the school has its own grounds which includes tennis courts. It was designed for 'Girls who earn their own living' who could obtain the best education at the lowest fee. Recently the building was subjected to a severe fire and completely lost its roof and sustained damage to the upper storeys. It has however been completely restored. (1906.)

134. The attraction of trams at the turn of the century (1905) is self evident, with attention also given to the photographer, who captures this record of children in Sidwell Street. Up until 1937 the section of the street which contained numbers 75 to 80 still stood but were eventually to be removed to make way for the Odeon Cinema. Sidwell Street contained many interesting Courts of which few exist today. These were Clodes Court, Exon Court, Porch Place, Trebles Court, Redlion Court. Townsend Court can still be seen today.

INTERIOR OF HALL, ST. HILDA'S SCHOOL, EXETER.

135. St. Hilda's School was established around 1880 and was one of the most eminent private schools in Exeter which catered solely for girls of all ages. It was both a day and boarding school. Situated in York Road, the main building had two houses adjoining it. In 1904 a large hall was built in the grounds for recreational use. In 1908 the principals were Mrs. Crabb and Miss Sanford.

136. Well dressed young ladies take advantage of the tennis court at St. Hilda's School. The new Hall, shown left, was erected in 1904.

137. The Pinhoe Road tram arrives at the junction of Old Tiverton Road and Blackboy Road. Hansome cabs could be taken into the City centre from this point. The horses patiently wait for the next customer. The large wooden structure was used by the police to carry out their duties. These were situated at various points in the city. Bedford Circus had its Police Box and also one was found at the Theatre Royal and stood in New North Road. The box was approximately 5 feet square and 8 feet high. A desk and a stool was inside and each box could hold about three people. Daily orders were received at each box and police officers signed on and off at these points. Meals would be taken at the box and this one catered for beat number 1 (St. Sidwells). Eventually the boxes were removed by the council and used for other purposes.

St. Sidwells, Exeter.

138. In the foreground stands the substantial horse trough donated to the City by Arthur Kempe. His name is inscribed on the base which supports a large ornamental shell. At a later date the trough was to be moved further back and now stands in a landscaped area beside St. Anne's Almshouses. At the immediate junction of both roads these delightful almshouses may still be seen. A tiny chapel is included within the group of houses and the whole dates back to around 1418. The houses were designed for eight poor people. Originally the home of a hermit, the site was changed into almshouses in 1561. St. Anne's Day was celebrated on July 26th. A ladder which appears to belong to the local fire brigade can be seen just outside the buildings.

137. The Pinhoe Road tram arrives at the junction of Old Tiverton Road and Blackboy Road. Hansome cabs could be taken into the City centre from this point. The horses patiently wait for the next customer. The large wooden structure was used by the police to carry out their duties. These were situated at various points in the city. Bedford Circus had its Police Box and also one was found at the Theatre Royal and stood in New North Road. The box was approximately 5 feet square and 8 feet high. A desk and a stool was inside and each box could hold about three people. Daily orders were received at each box and police officers signed on and off at these points. Meals would be taken at the box and this one catered for beat number 1 (St. Sidwells). Eventually the boxes were removed by the council and used for other purposes.

138. In the foreground stands the substantial horse trough donated to the City by Arthur Kempe. His name is inscribed on the base which supports a large ornamental shell. At a later date the trough was to be moved further back and now stands in a landscaped area beside St. Anne's Almshouses. At the immediate junction of both roads these delightful almshouses may still be seen. A tiny chapel is included within the group of houses and the whole dates back to around 1418. The houses were designed for eight poor people. Originally the home of a hermit, the site was changed into almshouses in 1561. St. Anne's Day was celebrated on July 26th. A ladder which appears to belong to the local fire brigade can be seen just outside the buildings.

139. On Wednesday October 6th, 1909 a grand historical pageant was held at Bury Meadow and was attended by large crowds of Exeter folk. The theme was 'Briton and Roman Exeter', as she might have been in AD 49 surrounded by palissades. The programme was as follows. A girl tending to sheep and a lad to the oxen. A Ronic altar is displayed. Children play with bows and arrows. From the City gate issues a procession of white robed druids with golden sickles. Bards follow with wreaths. A priestess and maidens surround the altar. An attack takes place on 'Isca' by the Roman army. A bloody battle takes place and the barbourous Exonians carry off some of the enemy into wattled enclosures. This grand event is attended by Roman chariots with splendid white horses. These delightful maidens were the attendants to the priestess.

140. With the beauty of the Devonshire countryside so close to the City, the residents have always had the privilege of enjoying this facility to the full at no extra cost. Here a couple, full of the joys of Spring, walk arm in arm in the sunshine up Rosebarn Lane. From the open fields at the top they would have enjoyed extremely fine views over the City, down the Exe Estuary and towards the open sea. Although those views still exist today, the open fields have now been taken over as a housing estate.